The Wave of Protests leading to Regimes Change in Africa: A Sociological Perspective

Ambrues M. Nebo Sr.

CIP a Camerei Naţionale a Cărţii

Nebo, Ambrues M.

The Wave of Protests leading to Regimes Change in Africa: A Sociological Perspective / Ambrues M. Nebo Sr. – Chişinău : Generis Publishing (Online Marketing Group), 2020 (Print on demand). – 44 p. : fot. color.

Referinţe bibliogr.: p. 39-43 şi în subsol.

ISBN 978-9975-153-46-1.

323.22:316.485.22(6)

N 32

Cover image: www.pixabay.com

Generis Publishing
Online orders: www.generis-publishing.com
Orders by email: info@generis-publishing.com

Table of Contents

ABSTRACT

From a sociological perspective, this book meticulously explored the wave of protests that changed three regimes (Algeria, Sudan, Zimbabwe) and ongoing regime change protests in Africa. It argued that the skepticism of trust in electoral system, skepticism of trust in independent Judiciary, the problem of majority rule and the conspicuous silence of the International Community (African Union, United Nations, ECOWAS, big world powers etc.) are the reasons behind the wave of protest for regime change in Africa. The crux of argument is premised on the questions that "How can protesters influence regime change through the ballot box; through constitutional courts whose credibility and independence remain questionable in Africa? This question derives from those opposing regimes change through protest as their position statement. ("Do it through the ballot box").

Finally, the paper concludes that no matter how much critics conceptualized this social phenomenon as unconstitutional that undermines Africa so-called young democracy, the continent remained vulnerable to social protest. Hence, social protest is theorized as the people limit of tolerance to continue to live with the products of bad governance believed to have failed them.

Key words: *Electoral System, People's power Regime Change, Social Protest,*

CHAPTER I

Introduction

Emerging social phenomena in human societies have always attracted the attention of Sociologists. It could be social, political, economic or religious, issues affecting societies. Sociologists must endeavor to proffer prescriptions to any social phenomenon affecting societies. One of the social phenomena deserving attention is the wave of social protests that led to prolonged regime change in some African countries and at the same time serving as the impetus for others to challenge and change the status quo. In recent times, sustained protest in Sudan, Algeria and Zimbabwe led to prolonged regime change. Recently in Liberia, a pressure group under the banner of the Council of Patriots seem to be motivated by the people power in these three countries. Despite appealed from some Liberians including the Liberia Churches of Council to disengage from the protest but wait for regime change through the ballot box, the Council of Patriots resolutely staged a mass protest on 6 January 2020 for President George Manneh Weah to fix the crumbling economy and address issues of alleged corruption or step down if he cannot fix the problems. Similarly, protest is ongoing to prevent proposed constitutional amendments to allow incumbent President Alpha Conde to run for a third term in office in Guinea, (The Guardian, 2019).

To proffer prescriptions to the wave of protests that many viewed as inimical to Africa post-independence growing democracy, it is essential that the reasons behind the phenomenon be known. Against this backdrop, this book examines the wave of these protests in Africa from a sociological perspective. It does so by structuring the book into three chapters. Chapter one briefly conceptualizes protest, Chapter two examines the normative or legal frameworks pertaining to protest. Particularly, it looks at the reliance for the protesters and citizens against regime change protests including the government in power. Chapter three briefly catalogues some of the protests that led to regime change in Africa including the most recent. It also explores the reasons behind the wave of protests in Africa. And finally, draws the conclusion with the way-forward as the prescriptions.

Conceptualizing Protest from a Sociological Perspective

A sociological perspective simply connotes the lenses employed to examine social phenomena within sociology as an academic discipline. The lenses consist of theoretical framework and conceptual framework postulated by prolific authors most of whom are accredited as pioneers of sociology. For example, (Karl Marx, Herbert Spencer, Georg Simme, Émile Durkheim, George Herbert Mead, C. Wright Mills, Max Weber, Robert Merton, etc.).

Many people viewed protest to be a political phenomenon. Of course, they are absolutely correct for thinking so. However, protest is not only confined to the Political Science as an academic discipline. It is a social phenomenon that impacts society. Because of this reason, protest has its place in sociology. It is called social protest. In the words of McLeod (2011), social protest is conceptualized as is a form of political expression that seeks to bring about social or political change by influencing the knowledge, attitudes, and behaviors of the public or the policies of an organization or institution. By political expression, it simply means people exercising their political rights guarantee by national and international laws that will be discussed as the legal frameworks under the chapter two of this book. The change could be policy reform, regime change, revolution etc. It is people driven phenomenon.

In sociology, protest is a form of collective behavior manifested by overt public displays, demonstration, civil disobedience, riot, petitions, boycotts, lobbying, sit-ins, marches, blockades, and strikes and various online activities. Unlike political science in which the protests have political position as their vested interests, it is totally different in sociology. Political positions or appointments as in power sharing deal are not the interest of the protesters. All they want is regime change. They are the ordinary people mostly affected by the behavior and actions of the government. They are people from diverse backgrounds from the society. They may include teachers, doctors, students, trade unions, labor unions, youth, etc. In most instances, some protests can escalate into violent confrontations even though the organizers do not intend it. The violence often arises due to riot police approach to the restrict, disperse or disassemble the crowd or protestors. This has been the cases of many violent protests in Africa especially the recent situation in Sudan (BBC News,2019), Guinea (The Guardian 2019), Burkina Faso (Frintz, 2014), etc. Social protest is defined as a form of collective behavior simply because, it usually involves large number of people who may not know each other but are emotionally focused on common purpose and done with upon accomplishment.

They can exist as an unstructured group without a nomenclature often influenced by opinion leaders, politicians, activist, etc, taking advantage of the people unmet needs. This kind of protest is generally short-lived that can impact society by making history. The regime changes in Sudan (BBC News, 2019), Algeria (Doubek, 2019), Zimbabwe (Torchia and Farai, 2017), Burkina Faso (Frintz, 2014), Egypt (Hardy, 2011), Tunisia (Davies, 2010) are example of this kind of social protest. They are the people power enshrined in constitutions and perhaps international law. Once the regime has changed, objective is met as such, the protest is over or done with.

They can also exist as structured group with nomenclature that is called social movement, another form of collective behavior defined as a highly structured organization with formally recognized leaders, and a deliberate attempt to institute societal change (Thomas, 1990). In Liberia, the Council of Patriots that staged the biggest protest on 7June 2019 caption 'Save the State' (Dodoo, 2019) and 6 January 2020 under the title 'President Weah step down'(Dopoe, 2020) is an example of social movement. By their numbers or size, they cannot provoke regime change. They rely on the down trodden masses believed to be affected by government action to stage protest. Without the masses coming out in their numbers, they are toothless bull dog or what in Liberia parlance called 'noise makers'.

Professor Neil Smelser outlined six preconditions that also applied to social protest as form or type of collective behavior. Because of their significance to the conceptualization of protest, it is important that this book briefly review each.

Structural Conduciveness: As the first precondition, it refers to the set-up or structure of a society or community that makes the protest possible? For example, the way in which the media especially radio talk show program propagates and polarize information about government can incite people already frustrated with the government to protest. In Liberia, the closure of Roots FM 102.7 owned by Henry Pedro Costa, a fearless talk show host known for criticizing government (Geterminah, 2019) is a classic example. In view of the government, the Costa show is using the media to incite people against the government evidenced by the September 24, 2019 'Bring back our money' protest. Despite the closure of the radio station, Roots FM 102.7 used MyTuner radio internet to convince people to turn out in their numbers for the 6 January 2020 'Step down protest against the President (Dopoe, 2020). Another contemporary example is the significant role of the social media in the "Arab Spring". It facilitated communication and interaction among protesters. Protesters used the social media to organize demonstration, disseminate information about their activities, and raise local and global awareness for the protest (Salem, Fadi; Mourtada, Rach, 2011).

Structural Strain: It refers to existing social conditions that put stress or strain on people and encourage them to take collective action as in protest. Example of social conditions include corruption, high unemployment, deprivation, discrimination, marginalization, bad policy, abuse of power that disadvantage majority of the people, lack of employment opportunities, etc. For example, monarchy, human rights violations, political corruption, economic decline, unemployment, concentration of wealth in the hands of monarchs in power for decades extreme poverty, and a number of demographic structural factors were the social conditions that led to series of anti-government protests, uprisings that changed regime in Tunisia, Egypt, Libya, Korotayev (2011).

In Liberia, the June 7 'Save the State' protest in which thousands of Liberians staged a peaceful protest in Monrovia, demanding the resignation of top government officials, and calling for government's actions in addressing the economic constraints and challenges confronting Liberians is another contemporary example.

Generalized Belief: It refers to what people believe is happening that cause them to take collective action as in protest, demonstration or civil disobedience. It can be argued that the way in which the government respond to the existing Structural Strain or social conditions enhance the people general belief that informed their decision for collective action. If they feel that the government is silent or insensitive to their concerns or doing little about the problem, protest as in any form become their viable option to draw government attention. As a contemporary example, the social conditions that existed for long period of time constituted the generalized belied that informed the reasons for the 'Arab Spring'. In Tunisia, Egypt, Libya majority of the people believed that authoritarian regime or rule was inimical to their survivability. They believe that regime change by protest will improve their conditions. Whether it happens or not, is not the focus of this paper. It is another topical issue that could be explored subsequently.

The April 14, 1979 'Rice Riot' that in some significance ways helped to end the 132 year of elite Americo-Liberia regime worth to be another practical example of generalized belief. The Progressive Alliance of Liberia that staged the protest managed to convinced the ordinary masses that the proposal was a self-aggrandizement, pointing out that Chenoweth and the Tolbert family of president William R. Tolbert operated large rice farms and would therefore, realize a tidy profit from the proposed price increase. The government argued that the proposed increased in the subsidized price of rice from $22 per 100-pound bag to $26 was intended to encourage rice farmers to stay on the land and produce rice for both subsistence crop and a cash crop, instead of abandoning their farms for jobs in the cities or on the rubber plantations, (Global Security, 2010). The wide gap of social inequality between the indigenes and the elite Americo-Liberians were one of the existing social conditions that informed the ordinary masses belief in the Progressive Alliance of Liberia for which they took to the street in Monrovia to protest.

Precipitating Factors: It refers to specific events that "trigger" the outbreak of collective behavior as in protest. As one of the reasons, it is not enough to explain the cause(s) of the protest. The structural strain defined as the existing social conditions are the root causes for protest. For contemporary example, the self-immolation of Tarek el-Tayeb Mohamed Bouazizi in response to the confiscation of his wares and the harassment and humiliation inflicted on him by a municipal official and her aides in 2010 was the main precipitating factor that sparked up the 'Arab Spring' in Tunisia. In Liberia, the way and manner in which the Police responded to the peaceful demonstration during the 1979 infamous 'Rice Riot' led to the violence.

Mobilization for Action: Refers to What do the people do? What specific actions to they take as part of their collective behavior as in social protest? Do they yell, scream, loot, block street, sit-in, set things on fire, destroy stuff? Or, do they head for the exits? What do they do? Using the April 14, 1979 infamous 'Rice Riot' in Liberia as example, the protesters looted from stores in Monrovia, destroy properties, clashed with the police by throwing stones. Similarly, in Burkina Faso 2015 protest that change the regime, protesters took to the street demanding the resignation of Blaise Compare, attacked Parliament building by setting it on fire. Protesting against Thursday's presidential election, protesters in Algeria took to the street in loud voice "No election with the gangs", "they must all be removed" and at the same time boycotted the election. According to the BBC news, they want all officials associated with the regime of ousted President Bouteflika to be removed from office, including interim President Abdelkader Bensalah and Prime Minister Nouredine Bedoui. All five candidates standing were closely linked with the rule of ex-President Bouteflika. In the Kabylie region, east of the capital, protesters stormed two polling centres. They destroyed ballot papers and boxes (Rouaba, 2019). Finally, in 2018, Protesters surrounded a bonfire on a street in demand for the release of Ugandan politician Robert Kyagulanyi (a.k.a. Bobi Wine) (Dionne,2018).

Social Control: At this point or stage in sequence, the protest can be controlled if mechanisms exist to prevent or minimize the situation. In other words, how do the government control and/or bring the situation under control? Do they send in security apparatus mainly riot police unit, National Television? In the opinion of this book, this is the critical stage. The manner in which the riot police unit tactically attempt to disperse the crowd often determined the dimension the protest will take. Without doubt, Africa is on record for using lethal repression for peaceful protest in Africa as the only mechanism believed to the best social control.

For example, in the April 14, 1979 infamous 'Rice Riot' in Liberia, the action of the Liberia National Police to use life bullet and tears gas as the option to disperse the crowd initially peaceful led to different dimension. Break down of social control immediately ensured. Looting, death and vandalization were the end results of police action. In Tunisia the police shot on protesters, Mubarak's regime in Egypt killed close to 1,000, Gaddafi's security forces killed protesters in Benghazi, as did the regimes Yemen, Syria and Bahrain (BBC News, 2013).

Finally, all of the protests in African politics especially the ones that led to regime change are manifestations of societal limits of tolerance to live and continue with the semblances of bad governance failing to meet the aspirations and expectations of the people who are custodian of power.

NORMATIVE FRAMEWORKS FOR THE WAVE PROTESTS IN AFRICA: WHO'S IN THE RIGHT, AND WHO'S IN THE WRONG?

The right for people to protest often referred to 'The People Power', 'Popular Sovereignty', 'The people greatest weapon' continued to attract debate in many democracies in Africa.

Primarily concerned about safety, national security and the protection of non-protesters fundamental rights to freedom of movement government have tried as much as they can to restrict, crackdown, disallowed any protect believing to be peaceful.

On the contrary, the actions of governments in Africa have always been supported by the Constitutions and international norms or laws. For example, government can invoke Article 11 of the African Charter on Human and Peoples Rights adopted in Nairobi June 27 and 1981 entered into force October 21, 1986 as the justification to restrict, prevent, disallow or crackdown on social protest. This same Article that recognizes individuals right to assembly freely also mandates

States party to the Charter to take measure in the interest of national security, the safety, heath, ethics and rights and freedom of others.

In the understanding of African governments, peaceful protest pose threat to national security, safety, health, ethics and rights to assembly freely. Similarly, government may invoke Article 21 the 1966 International Covenant on Civil and Political Rights as the justification to restrict social protest. In verbatim it says *"No restrictions may be placed on the exercise of this right other than those imposed in conformity with the law and which are necessary in a democratic society in the interests of national security or public safety, public order, the protection of public health or morals or the protection of the rights and freedoms of others."* All of these international provisions are also guaranteed by national Constitutions. For example, Article 58 (a) caption 'Functions of the President of the Republic' of the 2005 Sudan Constitution may be used by the President to restrict protest. It says *'preserve the security of the country and protect its integrity'*. In Guinea, the law recognizes protest but requires notification of the local authorities ahead of a proposed march or public meeting. The local authorities can prohibit a planned protest only if there is "a real threat to public order" (Human Right Watch, 2019). In Liberia despite article 17 of the constitution, government yet to establish legal provision saddled with the responsibility for national security and public order often insist or request that organizers of the protest must first seek a permit from the Ministry of Justice or the Liberia National Police. Moreover, the Liberia National Police reliance stems from Part III, Section 22.86 (A) of Liberia National Police Act of 2015, which is An Act to Amend Chapter 22, Subchapter D of the Act Amending the Executive Law of Liberia. In verbatim, it states "'Any person who desires to hold any special event in the form of demonstration, march, or similar event in any public place shall notify the County Attorney in the county where the event is to take place of his or her intention not less than seven days before the date of the special event"; (B) states: "Where the special event is to be held in Montserrado County, the notification shall be sent to the Minister [Justice] and consultations require by this section shall be with the Inspector General of Police". Unfortunately, this legal reliance is beneath the Constitution of Liberia. Precisely, it contravenes Article 2 (A) and (B) of the Constitution of Liberia which state:

(A) This Constitution is the supreme and fundamental law of Liberia and its provisions shall have binding force and effect on all authorities and persons throughout the Republic.

(B) Any laws, treaties, statutes, decrees, customs and regulations found to be inconsistent with it shall, to the extent of the inconsistency, be void and of no legal effect. The Supreme Court, pursuant to its power of judicial review, is empowered to declare any inconsistent laws unconstitutional. Without doubt, the current Liberia National Police Act 2015 as a regulation cannot survive any legal debate to restrict or prevent protest. The Government saddled with the responsibility for ensuring national security and public order may invoke both Article 11 of the African Charter on Human and People's Rights and Article 21 the 1966 International Covenant on Civil and Political Rights as the justifiable grounds to restrict or disallow social protest. Despite these clear provisions often employed by government in Africa, it is argued that there have been no universal condemnations for the social protest under the doctrine of popular sovereignty conceptualized as the people's power. The African Union (AU) stance on the wave of protest in Africa remain silent. It suggests recognition or endorsement sanctioned by its Charter on Human and People Rights and its Protocol on Good Governance and Democracy. This assertion is evidenced by AU silence or no condemnations on social protests. It only condemns brutal attacks on peaceful and armless protesters by State security apparatus. Moreover, the United Nations and other World Powers such as United States of America, Great Britain, also recognizes the people's power under the doctrine of popular sovereignty.

In the view of the protesters, their rights to protest against any appalling conditions that threaten their survivability is guaranteed by both international and national instruments. It is a global social phenomenon deeply rooted in every Country political culture that cannot be aloof from legal instrument. Article 21 of1966 International Covenant on Civil and Political Rights clearly confer this right upon the people. It states, *"The right of peaceful assembly shall be recognized"*. Mindful of government calculated attempt to suppress this right, it cautions against any form of restriction. It states: *"No restrictions may be placed on the exercise of this right other than those imposed in conformity with the law and which are necessary in a democratic society in the interests of national security or public safety, public order (ordre public), the protection of public health or morals or the protection of the rights and freedoms of others"*. Similarly, Article 11 of the AU Charter on Human and People Rights conferred upon the people their right to protest. It states "Every individual shall have the right to assemble freely with others. The exercise of this right shall be subject only to necessary restrictions provided for by law in particular those enacted in the interest of national security, the Safety, heath, ethics and rights and freedom of others. The phrase 'No restriction may be placed on the exercise of this right', does not give protest an absolute right. Restriction becomes necessary when the ongoing protest from all indications pose serious and significant threat to national security. However, these conditions do not give any government the right to restrict the people right based on insinuation that the protest pose will threaten national security. Of course, these instruments also take cognizance of the fundamental rights of non-protesters or those not directly or actively involved in the protest. This in no way gives any government the grounds to still restrict the right to protests. Instead, the government through its relevant security apparatus must ensure protection for all. Nationally, the Constitutions of almost all the Countries in Africa conferred the right to protest (peace assembly) upon the people as the custodian of political power. For example, Article 17 of the 1986 Liberian Constitution states *"All persons, at all times, in an orderly and peaceable manner, shall have the right to assemble and consult upon the common good, to instruct their representatives, to petition the Government or other functionaries for the redress of grievances and to associate fully with others or refuse to associate in political parties, trade unions and other organizations."*

Article 10 of the 2010 Guinea Constitution also conferred upon the people the right to protest. It states *"All citizens have the right of demonstration [manifestation] and of procession [cortège]"*.

Similarly, Article 41 under chapter IV caption: Rights and liberties of the 1989 amended version of the Constitution of the People's Democratic Republic of Algeria in 1996 conferred upon the people of Algeria the right to protest. In verbatim, it states "Freedom *of expression, association and meeting are guaranteed to the citizen"*. Finally, Article 40 of the 2005 Sudan Constitution also conferred upon the people of Sudan the right to protest. In verbatim it states *"The right to peaceful assembly shall be guaranteed; every person shall have the right to freedom of association with others, including the right to form or join political parties, associations and trade or professional unions for the protection of his interests"*.

The right to protest that is not necessarily violent or a threat to the interests of national security or public safety is a manifestation or expression of popular sovereignty enshrined in almost all of the Constitutions in Africa. For example, Chapter 1 of the 2005 Sudan Constitution, sub title Sovereignty conferred upon the right of popular sovereignty. It states *"The sovereignty of the nation is vested in its people and shall be exercised in accordance with the provisions of this Constitution and the law"*.

Similarly, Chapter III, Article 6 of the 1989 amended version of the Constitution of the People's Democratic Republic of Algeria in 1996 conferred upon the people of Algeria the power popular sovereignty. It states *"The people are the source of any power. The national sovereignty belongs exclusively to the People"*. Article 2 of the 2010 Guinea Constitution also conferred upon the people of Guinea the power of popular sovereignty. It states *"The national sovereignty belongs to the People who exercise it by their elected representatives or by way of referendum. No individual, no fraction of the People may arrogate its exercise. Sovereignty is exercised in accordance with this Constitution which is the supreme Law of the State"*.

Article 1 of the 1986 Liberia Constitution also conferred upon the people of Liberia the power of popular sovereignty. It states *"All power is inherent in the people. All free governments are instituted by their authority and for their benefit and they have the right to alter and reform the same when their safety and happiness so require. In order to ensure democratic government which responds to the wishes of the governed, the people shall have the right at such period, and in such manner as provided for under this Constitution, to cause their public servants to leave office and to fill vacancies by regular elections and appointments"*.

It is no doubt that all of the legal provisions cited legitimize social protest as an expression of popular sovereignty. However, these specific provisions are very clear about regime change. It specifies election as the only prescription for regime change based upon dissatisfaction in the social contract theory pustulated by notable social thinkers such as John Locke, Thomas Hobbes, Jean-Jacques Rousseau that reserves the power of revolt for the people in case they are dissatisfied with the institutional arrangements put in place (Laskar, 2013).

In other words, election results reflecting the majority votes are expression of popular sovereignty for any regime change. However, the biggest question that begs for answer is why the people do not want to invoke this constitutional provision (Elections) to effect regime change for whatever reasons seem to be genuine? Under chapter 2 of this book, I proffer the argument as the reasons.

CATALOGUE OF REGIME CHANGE PROTESTS IN AFRICA

This section in sequence catalogues some of the protests that led to regime change in Africa and ongoing protest for regime change. I began with the so-called Arab

Spring that resulted in regime changes in countries such as Tunisia, Egypt and Libya.

Following the death of a Tunisian street vendor Mohammed Bouazizi set himself on fire to protest the arbitrary seizing of his vegetable stand by police over failure to obtain a permit in 2010, Tunisians in their thousands took to the street to express their limit of tolerance through protest against the 20 years authoritarian rule of president Zine El Abidine Ben Ali that later resigned and exiled to Saudi Arabia in early January 2011, Davies, (2010). It is now referred to as the 'Jasmine Revolution. The effects of the Tunisian Revolution spread strongly to five other countries: Libya, Egypt, Yemen, Syria and Bahrain.

Flashed back: Protesters assembled in Tunis 2010

Courtesy of (Asia News/Agencies, 2010)

Flashed back: Protesters in Tahrir Square during the protest in 2011

Courtesy of Cairo (AsiaNews, 2011)

Inspired by similar reasons that led to regime change in Tunisia, thousands of Egyptian as shown in the above flashback photo beginning from 25 January 2011 assembled at Tahrir square to demand the resignation of the prolonged regime of authoritarian rule of president Hosni Mubarak. On the 18 day of the sustained protest (11 February 2011) Mubarak steps down thus ending his almost 30 years rule, Hardy (2011).

Flashed back: Thousands of protesters gathered in Bayda 2011

Courtesy of BBC News (2011)

As shown in the above flashback, the same inspiration that thousands of Egyptians took from the Tunisian uprising also took over thousands of Libyans on 15 February 2011.Despite government aggressive attempt to repelled the protest that spread to Tripoli demanding the end of the 42 years authoritarian regime of Colonel Muammar Gaddafi. The protest continued until 20 October 2011, Gaddafi regime came to an end following his capture and assassination by his captors in Sirte, Libya, Parks (2011).

Flashed back of 2014 protest in Burkina Faso

Courtesy of BBC News (2011)

Maybe inspired by the Arab Spring, 1n 2014 Blaise Campaore was chased from office by a popular uprising after he proposed changing term limits to extend his presidency for another five years that could have added to the 27 years rule in power.

Under this section, recent protests that led to regime changes and other pertaining to regime change are briefly highlighted.

ALGERIA

Flashed back: Protesters assembled in Algiers 2019.

Courtesy of Ryad Kramdi-AFP 2019

As shown in the above flashed back, in February, after President Abdelaziz Bouteflika announced his intent to run for a fifth term, an estimated 3 million protesters took to the street in Algiers to demand complete end to his 20 years rule that failed to meet the aspiration and expectation of the masses. On 3 April 2019, Bouteflika finally succumbed to popular sovereignty pressure, Doubek (2019). Despite the resignation of Bouteflika, the people in their thousands continue to invoke Article of 41 of their Constitution protesting against officials associated with the regime of ousted President Bouteflika to be removed from office, including interim President Abdelkader Bensalah and Prime Minister Nouredine Bedoui. More importantly, five of the candidates in the election believed to be associated with the Bouteflika regime especially Mr Bensalah and Mr Bedoui that cannot be trusted to secure a free and transparent election because they have benefitted from former President Bouteflika's rule, Rouaba (2019).

Flashed back: Protesters assembled in Khartoum, Sudan, 2019

Courtesy of New York Times 2019

In late December 2018, President Bashir's government imposed emergency austerity measures to try to stave off economic collapse. The measures cut bread and fuel subsidies. Inspired by popular uprising in Algeria, the masses in Sudan invoked Article 40 of the 2005 amended Constitution demanding an end to the 30 rules of President Omar al-Bashir. The Military took advantage of the people sustained protest to overthrow Bashir in April 2019 (BBC News 2019) The masses demanded that the military turn over power to interim civilian government. Following the African Union sanction attempt and condemnations from the United Nations, the Military finally relinquish power to interim civilian government made of 18-member cabinet led by Prime Minister Abdalla Hamdok, which includes four women. The interim civilian government is expected to steer the daily affairs of the country during a transition period of 39 months (France24, 2019).

Flashed back: Protesters calling for Mugabe impeachment in Harare

Courtesy of Ben Curtis- 2017

Following sustained weeks of protests by thousands of Zimbabweans, overwhelming pressure from the military to put him under house arrest and at the same time lawmakers from his ruling party and opposition who started impeachment proceedings, Robert Mugabe finally succumbed to pressures by resigning in 2017 thus ending his 37 years rule in power, Torchia & Mutsaka (2017).

Protesters Assembled in Banjul, Gambia

Courtesy of Mustapha K Darboe 2019

A pro-democracy movement in Gambia invoked Article 25 under Chapter IV of the Gambia Constitution when they took to the streets on 16 December 2019 calling for President Adama Barrow to resign and organize fresh votes.

Protesters from "3 years jotna" (it's now 3 years) held a procession at the outskirt of Banjul, from Sting Corner to Denton Bridge, where they delivered a letter to Ebrima Sankareh, the spokesperson of the government.

Barrow came to power on the backing of seven political parties and three independent candidates. The coalition agreement was to serve a three-year transitional term and leave to hold an election in which he will not contest, Darboe (2019).

Protesters took to the street in Conakry while carrying Flag 2019

Courtesy of Cellou Binani/AFP via Getty Images 2019

Following instruction from President Alpha Condé, to the Prime Minister Ibrahima Fofana in September 2019 to initiate consultation pertaining to the possibility to amend the Constitution that will the President to run for a third term in office, hundreds of thousands of Guineans have invoked Article 10 of the 2010 Guinea Constitution by taken to the streets protesting against the prospect of Condé running for a third term. They chanted the Susu phrase for *"this will not happen"*, the slogan of the protest movement, and burn car tyres. Many wore red T-shirts, armbands, hats and bandanas – the colour of the opposition coalition Front National Pour La Défense De La Constitution (FNDC). (The Guardian, 2019) Alpha Condé, has been in power since the country's first democratic elections in 2010, winning a second five-year term. His second term and final five-year term ends in 2020.

At least 20 civilians were killed in the unrest including one gendarme (The Guardian, 2019).

Thousands gathered at Capitol Hill to protest falling economy in Liberia

Courtesy of Krippahl and Seagbeh – 6 Jan 2020

Recently on 6 January 2020, a pressure group under the banner of Council of Patriots (COP) who staged one of the biggest peaceful protest in post conflict Liberia "Save the State" 7 June 2019, staged another mass protest on Capitol Hill, the seat of the government in Monrovia, (Krippahl & Seagbeh 2020). The COP citing Article 17 of the 1986 Constitution as their legal reliance argued that until President Weah address the "Save the State" petitions presented to the government on 7 June 2019, they will remain on the grounds of the Capitol Hill. The Liberia National Police fired tear gas and a water cannon to clear peaceful protesters against the orders for cooking evening meals perceived as threat to public safety, the Capitol building and the Executive Mansion. (Al Jazeera and News agencies, 2020).

On the premise that the George Weah-led administration is proceeding wrongly on governance, the petitions in summary called upon the government to address issues such as the poor economy, alleged corruption, lack of transparency, accountability and dismissal and prosecution of few government officials especially Minister of Finance and State.

CHAPTER II

THE WAVE OF PROTESTS IN AFRICA

Without dismissing or countering reasons such as corruption, Intransigence on the part of leaders and norm-breaking and its far-reaching consequences argued by some prolific experts in African politics, this book opinionate or opine the below reasons why Africa will continue to face social protest leading to regime change.

SKEPTICISM OF TRUST IN ELECTORAL SYSTEM

People who genuinely opposed protest for regime change in Africa because of its implications continue to argue that the ballot box as legitimized by constitutional provision is the best prescription to effect regime change failing to meet the aspiration and expectation of the people. Of course, this argument is valid. However, why the recent protests in Algeria, Sudan, Zimbabwe, and even the Arab Spring did not invoke their respective constitutional provisions to effect regime change? Why people in the Gambia, Guinea and Liberia do not want to use the ballot box to effect regime change believed to have failed the masses' expectations? These are hard core questions that deserve our attentions. Could it mean that the people are skeptical that using the ballot box will not change the regime? If this is the case, then it suggests that those protesting for regime change outside the ballot box do not trust the democratic process. The most recent examples of elections irregularities can be seen from the following cases in three African Countries:

The controversial elections results in which South African president Cyril Ramaphosa and other international Stakeholders urged Congolese to accept a fraudulent election result in the name of "consolidating democracy", Gathara (2019).

The 2015 Sudan elections scheduled for 2 April, but were delayed by eleven days in which Omar al-Bashir won the presidential election by a landslide amid a boycott from the majority of the opposition, (BBC News, 2015).

The 2016 Equatorial Guinea elections amid boycott citing that the election would be "anti-constitutional" and that Obiang would win "with a big score as a result of fraud". Incumbent President Teodoro Obiang Nguema Mbasogo retained his office with 93.7 percent of the vote, (Africanews, 2016).

From all indications, these examples raise the issues of trust in these countries electoral system? It is no doubt that Africa remain on record for fraudulent elections in favor of incumbent Presidents. A survey conducted in 2016/2017 by Afrobarometer, a pan-African, non-partisan research network may validate the assertion of skepticism of public trust in electoral system. According to the report that examined public trust in 47 countries, only half of Africans trust their national electoral commissions, and many fear violence and unfair practices during election campaigns, (Kerr & Lührmann, 2017). Another report highlighted that while public assessments vary widely by country, on average more than four in 10 Africans express serious concerns about the fairness of vote counts, corruption during elections, and the safety of voters. Half of Africans say elections don't work well to ensure that voters' views are represented or that elected officials can be held accountable. (Afrobarometer Round 6, 2016).

Whether the statistics or data gathered from Afrobarometer survey maybe exaggerated that questions its validity, one cannot deny the fact that Africa is not on record for fraudulent elections perpetuating prolonged regime.

Peter Penar is a researcher and PhD candidate in the Department of Political Science, Michigan State University argued that because one-third of Africans think that votes in elections are always counted fairly in which disputed poll has been a flash point for protests, it diminishes the public's faith in the democratic processes, Penar (2016). With this kind of situation, how can you encourage protesters to use the ballot box to effect regime change? What is the guarantee that the process will be transparent? Inarguably, all of the prolonged regime characterized by repression, suppression, dictatorship, etc are connected to fraudulent election results. Take case of President Teodoro Obiang Nguema Mbasogo who has been in power since 1979 that won elections controversially, do you expect democratic election to change his regime if not protest soon to come? What's about Yoweri Museveni of Uganda who has been in power since 1986 that also scarped the constitutional provision to extend presidential term limit to perpetuate his regime? Museveni has controversially won all of the elections. The most recent 2011 election was criticized by European Union and United States for the election for lack of transparency and detentions of opposition candidates (Global Post/AFP, 2016). What's the expectation for regime change through the ballot box if not popular uprising through social protest that seems to be imminent? Take the case of President Paul Biya, who has been ruling Cameroon since 1982 wining all of the elections controversially. The most recent was the 2018 elections in which the Constitutional Council declared

President Paul Biya the winner of the presidential election for his seventh term, Signé (2018). Again, what's the expectation for regime change through the ballot box if not imminent protest? Take the case of the recent 2010 elections in Burundi in which president, Pierre Nkurunziza, was elected amid boycott by opposition parties and massive fraud by Nkurunziza party, Khadiagala (2011). With all of these examples of fraudulent elections, how can those opposing protest for regime change in Africa expect the people to patiently wait for the ballot box? What is the guarantee that incumbents will not rig election results in their favor? So, until African leaders can instil trust and confidence in our electoral system, the people will invoke both the power of international law and constitutional provisions as their reliance to protest for regime change. No matter how other see and interprets their actions as unconstitutional, until African leaders can instil credibility in the electoral system that will significantly reduce the skepticism of trust in the electoral system, the people regardless of the implications will continue to resort to the use of popular sovereignty through protest for regime change.

SKEPTICISM OF TRUST IN THE JUDICIAL SYSTEM

Most often Courts are at the centre of critical election disputes, corruption cases concerning political elites and judicial review of controversial legislation. As such, their independence remains crucial not only for maintaining a democratic culture but the trust and confidence of the people. Judicial independence is deeply rooted in the doctrine of separation of power and of check and balance. The French philosopher Montesquieu and the American statesmen Madison articulates that the separation of powers stems from the belief that "the best way to control government power is to divide it among the various branches of government — the legislative, executive and judicial branches" Montesquieu and Madison (1788). The judiciary plays a crucial role in the system of checks and balances, a role which demands independence from the executive and legislature. Any form of perceived interference undermines the independence of courts.

Consequently, citizens and even the international community will view the independence of the court with serious skepticism. When this happens, integrity and trust become questionable.

In theory, it can be argued that Courts are independent of the executive and legislature. However, in practice, copious evidences have shown that political interference from the executive have raised eyebrows on the independence of the Courts in Africa.

Given this phenomenon, what's the guarantee that the Court will not rule in favor of the incumbent? In as much as the people view the Courts with serious skepticism, it becomes needless to go through the ballot box to effect regime change in Africa.

Take the case of the recent 2018 election in Cameroon in which the Constitutional Court declared Paul Biya as the winner after adjudicating controversial results filed by opposition party (Kindzeka, 2018).

Regarding the case of the constitutional court of the Democratic Republic of the Congo that declared Felix Tshisekedi winner of presidential election viewed as the favourite successor of Joseph Kabila? The DRC's constitutional court was widely seen as beholden to Kabila, who was in power since his father assassination in 2001, (Guardian, 2019). In the case of Malawi's top court ruling in the 2019 highly controversial elections in which opposition leaders led by Lazarus Chakwera and Saulos Chilima alleged that the election was rigged by altering results sheets using correction fluid. The court declared the Incumbent President Peter Mutharika of the Democratic Progressive Party as the winner, (Al Jazeera, 2019). With respect to the case of Liberia in which the current ruling party majority law makers and their affiliates impeached Associate Justice Janneh Kabineh for his independent and dissenting opinion contrary to the views of his colleagues pertaining to the controversial election results filed by the Liberty party in 2017. Even though Justice Janneh opinion was not among the counts that led to his impeachment presided over by the Chief Justice, however many legal pundits and some prominent opinion leaders viewed the impeachment as unconstitutional and politically motivated by the executive because of his contrary opinion, Dodoo (2019). The executive in line with constitutional provision nominated Judge Yusuf Kaba who was subsequently confirmed by the Senate as Associate Chief Justice of the Supreme Court. Similarly, in Liberia, President George Weah immediately replaced Stipendiary Magistrate Ernes F.B. Bana of the Monrovia City Court, whose ruling on November 4, 2019 disagreed with argument by government lawyers in the writ to close-down the Roots FM 102.7 radio station owned by talk-show host Henry Pedro Costa, Davis (2019). Though it is not clear whether the President replacement of Magistrate Ernes F.B. Bana was due to his judicial indiscretion, given the criticality of Roots FM 102.7 on the way the government is proceeding mainly the president, it is difficult to rule out the possibility.

With these kinds of scenarios, is it not a caveat to the judiciary especially judges and Magistrate that can be replaced by the President? Thinkably, it is an attack on the independence of the Judiciary? The same way Africa remain on the records for fraudulent elections, so it remains on records for perceived political interference mainly from the executive irrefutably seen as political demigod. It can also be argued that some of the prolonged regimes in Africa got their legitimacy from constitutional courts' ruling. Consider the case of the recent 2018 election in Cameroon in which Cameroon's Constitutional Council declared Paul Biya as the winner after adjudicating controversial results filed by opposition parties is one of the classic examples. On the basis of insufficient evidence, the Cameroon's Constitutional Council threw out 18 petitions filed by opposition leaders Maurice Kamto, Joshua Osih and others demanding the election be nullified, Kindzeka (2018). In this kind of situation, how it is possible for people to change the regime through the constitutional court often influenced by the executive? Can regime change in Equatorial Guinea be anticipated through the constitutional court? How many opposition parties have won elections cases through constitutional courts, how many constitutional courts have ruled against incumbent Presidents for controversial elections results filed by oppositions? Arguably, any existence as in the case of Malawi top court ruled to overturn the 2019 presidential vote after the opposition argued that the vote was rigged (Africanews, 2019) could be an isolated case. Therefore, until the people can trust the independence of the constitutional courts, protests for regime change will remain as a disturbing social phenomenon in Africa.

THE PROBLEM OF MAJORITY RULE

This may sound too strange to be one the reasons behind the wave of protests for regime change in Africa. Let me elucidate how it is one of the factors. To begin with, majority rule as in theory is presumed to be the will of the people through their elected representatives. So, it means that the people must support and respect decision based upon majority rule. Africa is on record for rebellious through protest against decision made by majority. It is a complete contradiction. The case of Burkina Faso in 2014 that led to the protest that unseat and exiled Blaise Compare and even the ongoing protest in Guinea are classic examples worth noting. Uganda, Rwanda, Cameroon etc. are also good examples that worth to predict protest at a given time. Let's take a scanty look at Burkina Faso. In 2014, Blaise Compare through the majority of Parliament members from the ruling party attempted to scarp the constitutional term limits for another five years that could have if succeeded added to his 27 years rule in power. Ironically, this attempt presumed to be in the interest of the masses since it was in the majority provoked a violent remonstration that led to regime change. Similarly, violent protest is ongoing in Guinea due to instruction from President Alpha Conde through the Prime Minister to draft a new or amend constitutional provision for his third term in office. According to Guinea constitution, his final five-year term expires in 2020 but the 81-year-old leader has refused to rule out running again, Samb (2019). Now the question worth asking is why the people in their hundreds of thousands through protest resisted the attempt by the government to amend the constitutional provision of the presidential term limit? A possible guest could be based upon perceived fear that parliament will act on majority rule presumably believed to be in the interest of the people on grounds that they represent them. If this happens, one cannot rule out the possibility for election results rigging in favor of the incumbent. Given this kind of situation, do you expect that the ballot box will affect regime change? Also, with regard to the case of Equatorial Guinea in which Teodoro Obiang Nguema, who has been in power since 1979, pushed through a referendum that changed the constitution in 2011 to allow him for re-election after age 75. The changes also allow Obiang to handpick his successor. Consider the case of Cameroon in which President Paul Biya, in power since 1982, was barred by a two-term limit from running again in 2011 but got legislators to remove all term limits from the constitution in 2008 despite violent protests. In the case of President Yoweri Museveni of Uganda, who once said that "no African head of a state should be in power for more than 10 years," has ironically governed since 1986. In 2005 he succeeded in getting the constitution changed to scrap all term limits, Guliyev (2009). In these situations, can the possibility for imminent remonstration for regime change be ruled out? Finally, in these situations, what's the possibility that the ballot box will affect regime change if not imminent remonstration or social protest?

Any majority rule that scarps presidential term limits is tantamount to violation of the concept popular sovereignty. In other words, how can the outcome of majority rule believed to reflect popular sovereignty or the people power be greeted with counter reaction through social protest? It is not a contradiction?

Conspicuous Silence of the International community

Coupled with international normative frameworks, it is no doubt that international condemnations mainly from the African Union, United Nations, ECOWAS, and other Super powers significantly helped to eliminate coup d'état that once threaten Africa young democracy. Article 4h of the AU's Constitutive Act condemns and rejects all unconstitutional changes of government and also gives the group the right to intervene in a member state under "grave circumstances". This is the AU reliance to reject all forms of coup d'état. Recently the world witnessed the African Union condemnation of Military takeover in Sudan following sustained protest and threated sanction precisely suspension of Sudan membership from the AU. Similarly, the military takeover in Zimbabwe also came under sharp condemnation following President Robert Gilbert Mugabe resignation. In the case of protests that led to regime change, one would expect the same reaction from AU as it did for military takeover on grounds that regime change resulting from sustained protest is viewed by many as unconstitutional. They argued that the resignation or step down of the president is not voluntary but involuntary due to pressure from sustained popular uprising. Despite this argument that could be valid, the AU continue to remain conspicuously silent about regime protest. In other words, the international community is yet to condemn popular uprising. What remain cleared is the condemnation on lethal repression on protesters or peaceful protesters by State security apparatus. To me this conspicuous silence by the international community suggests endorsement for regime change protest. Maybe the reason(s) could stem from the AU normative framework that recognizes the right to assemble freely with others. Another reason for the conspicuous silence could be based upon the fact the protesters are not politicians interested in positions. What interests them is to change the regime believed to have failed them. Maybe what could be conceptualized as soft power employed by the protesters is far from hard power conceptualized as treasonable and unconstitutional. Therefore, until the international community can reject and condemn the people power or popular sovereignty (protest for regime change) as it did for military takeover, the people will hold unto the inclination that regime change protest is legal and endorsed. A classic example can be seen from the recent statement from one of the most influential United States Lawmaker Rep. Chris Smith that called on the Liberian government to ensure respect for the mass public demonstration that transpired 6 January 2020 intended for President Weah to step down. He further cautions the government that violation of this fundamental right will attract "Global Magnitsky Sanction" Sieh (2019). Carefully note that Rep. Smith directly endorse the action of the Council of Patriots. Trust me, had Rep. Smith said anything negative against the planned mass demonstration, it would have signalled condemnation. Whether he says it or not, to any reasonable person, it is an impetus for the protest especially coming a from lawmaker of one of the biggest super power in global politics.

APPLICATION OF NEIL J. SMELSER THEORY TO THE WAVE OF PROTESTS IN AFRICA

As the crux of this book, this sub-title applies professor Neil J. Smelser (1963) theory as the main framework for the analysis of the wave of protests that the led to regime changes and the prospects for more regime change protests in Africa. From sociological analysis, skepticism of trust in electoral system, the judicial system and the problem of majority rule can be likened to "Structural Conduciveness" articulated by professor Smelser (1963). It is about what set-up or structure of a society or community that makes the outbreak of collective behavior possible? As earlier explained in the book, social protest is a form of collective behavior. The question worth asking is, what structure of the African society is setting up social protest? Nothing but the conduct of election commission, the independence of the judiciary, precisely the constitutional court coupled with the parliament use of majority rule have raised eyebrows of people skepticism of trust these structures (Election Commission, Constitutional Courts or Judiciary, Parliament) that embodies the African society.

Connected to structural conduciveness likens to skepticism of trust in elector system, Judicial system and the problem of majority rule is "Structural Strain" considered as the second pre-condition for collective behavior. The connection between these structures and structural strain may sounds strange. Conceptualized as social conditions that motivate collective behavior as in social protest, protesters demanding regime change are pushed by any of the following factors bordering on bad governance that threatens their livelihood or survivability. Rampant corruption affecting infrastructure development, economic hardship, alarming unemployment rate, etc. It is no doubt that trust and confidence in these structures are extremely critical to changing the regime that failed to address the semblances of bad governance. Therefore, if the electoral process, judicial system and Parliament are not credible, it is most likely that aggrieved citizens will take advantage of popular sovereignty through social protest instead of waiting patiently for the ballot box that in most instances or cases retain the incumbent regime people dissatisfied with. In summation, the skepticism of trust in these structures that create grounds for structural conduciveness are extremely connected to social strain. About generalized belief as the third pre-condition, it is also connected to the skepticism of trust in electoral system, judicial system and the problem of majority rule. Arguably, there is a relationship between generalized belief and perception. What people see and hear often influence their perceptions especially supported by how they interpret what is been seen and heard. Remember that general perception regarding people trust in Africa electoral system or election commission bodies surveyed by Afrobarometer 1n 2016/2017 cited in this book. According to the report that examined public trust in 47 countries, only half of Africans trust their national electoral commissions, and many fear violence and unfair practices during election campaigns, (Kerr & Lührmann, 2017). If we subtract the half of Africans that trust their national electoral commissions, it clearly implies that majority of the respondents surveyed do not trust their national electoral commissions. With this kind of generalized belief, how can protesters be encouraged to effect regime change through the ballot box? The fourth pre-condition articulated by Sociologist Smelser is "Precipitating Factors". It is about specific events that "trigger" the outbreak of collective behavior as in social protest. How can this pre-condition be applied to skepticism of trust in electoral system? What's the connection? If people already believed their national election commission not to be credible, the declaration of the election winner by the election commission can provoke a protest against the incumbent or winner. This is no doubt in Africa elections replete with social protests that question the legitimacy of the regime. For example, the 2019 Benin election in which the protesters clashed with police in post-election violence due to the electoral commission's pronouncement of provisional results which had been held without a single opposition candidate. Due to new eligibility criteria that barred opposition parties from fielding candidates in parliamentary elections, results showed that over three-quarters of the country's five million registered voters heeded the call from the Opposition leaders to abstain from voting. The protesters demanded the step down of President Patrice Talon, (News Central 2019). Similarly, in Malawi 2019 election, protesters demanded the resignation of electoral body chairperson, Jane Ansah following his declaration of incumbent President Peter Mutharika as the winner. The protesters believed that Malawi Electoral Commission mismanaged the results in favor of the incumbent President, Xinhua (2019). These examples and many more yet to be mentioned are not to establish the rightness of the protesters, but to explain the skepticism of trust in electoral commission especially appointed by the incumbent. Not necessarily means credibility issues, the power to appoint election commissioners could be one of the arguable reasons for people skepticism of trust in elections. Finally, the declaration of election winner that in some cases trigger social protest is not enough reason that explain the cause of the protest, but rather, the generalized belief of skepticism of trust in electoral system. The fifth pre-condition articulated by Sociologist Smelser is "Mobilization for Action". Remember, it refers to What do the people do? What specific actions to they take as part of their collective behavior? Applying this pre-condition to the skepticism of trust in electoral system, the obvious answer is social protest. The question that begs for answer(s) is what drives the people mobilization for action? Or what cause the people to mobilize their actions in the form of social protest? Obviously the skepticism of trust in the electoral system, judicial system and the problem of majority rule equated to structural conduciveness that offers no remedies to the multiplicity of problems equated to social strains are the answers. Recall the case of Burkina Faso in which parliament acted on the basis of majority rule to scarp the constitutional provision in favor of Blaise Compaoré. The recent protest in Guinea in 2019 is another classic example of majority rule that prompted the people to mobilize their actions through social protest. Finally, the six precondition is "Social Control". As a reminder, it is about how do the government control or bring the situation under control? As always the case, riot police or para-military apparatus are legally employed to control the situation. This is extremely critical to the survivability of the regime in power. In most instances, it has forced the regime to relinquish power. The case of Robert Mugabe of Zimbabwe, Omar Hassan Ahmad al-Bashir of Sudan, Abdelaziz Bouteflika of Algeria, Hosni Mubarak of Egypt, Blaise Compaoré from Burkina Faso etc, are some of the classic examples of African leaders forced to resign from power due to the manner in which their respective security apparatus control social protest. Under social control, there is a question that also begs for answer. What prompts social control? The obvious answer is social protest caused by the skepticism of trust in the electoral system, judicial system and the problem of majority rule equated to structural conduciveness that also connected to social strains and mobilization for action. So, it is clearly seen how one pre-condition leads to another.

CHAPTER III

CONCLUSION

Mindful of the already political and economic fragilities of most African countries that may get worsen by protest for regime change, the opinion discussed in this paper does not necessarily suggests support for this social phenomenon. The manifest intent is to help proffer prescriptions to the wave of protest conceptualized as one of the contemporary predicaments faced by the African societies squarely attributed to our political leaders' quest for power. The wave of protest is a manifestation of the people's power that speaks volume of their dissatisfaction with the regime. Those on the opposing side of protest for regime change conceptualized it as unconstitutional that must be discouraged but careless about the causes. To discourage the wave of protest for regime change, enough care for the reasons discussed in this paper must attract the attention of the continent. These reasons are: Skepticism of trust in electoral system, Skepticism of trust in Judicial System The problem of majority Rule and Conspicuous Silent of the International community. In the opinion of this paper, no amount of counter reactions as in rebuttal, rejection or crackdown will stop the people power backed by both international and national laws. Moreover, no government can withstand the people power through protest as recently experienced in Algeria, Sudan, Zimbabwe, Burkina Faso. Its' end result couple with the conspicuous silence by the international community has become the impetus for others facing similar problems to challenge the status quo.

Until the visible and undisputed causes are taken seriously and address, the continent will continue to experience more protests for regime change. It is the people's limits of tolerance to live with bad governance responsible for their never-ending socioeconomic conditions. They don't care about the implications protest for regime change will bring. All they want is an end to the regime that failed them.

Finally, protest that led to regime changes is a lesson for incumbent and mainly successors to take cue from. It is caveat for prolonged regime in Africa that have not done so much for the people whose power being used to benefit the interest of the few elites.

BIBLIOGRAPHY

Africanews (2016), "Equatorial Guinea heads to the polls on Sunday". Retrieved 2016-04-24.

Africanews (2019) Malawi court nullifies presidential election results, orders fresh poll. https://www.africanews.com/2020/02/03/malawi-court-nullifies-presidential-election-results-orders-fresh-poll//. Accessed 25 July 2020

Al Jazeera (2019), Malawi's top court hears presidential election result challengehttps://www.aljazeera.com/news/2019/08/malawi-top-court-hears-presidential-election-result-challenge-190808160542846.html Accessed 21 Dec 2019.

Al Jazeera and News agencies (2020) Liberian police fired tear gas, water cannon to clear protesters. https://www.aljazeera.com/news/2020/01/liberians-protest-worsening-economic-situation-200106134145168.html. Accessed 21 Dec 2019

Afrobarometer News Release (2016) Election quality, public trust are central) issues as African nations look toward next contests (Afrobarometer findings)

BBC News (2013), Arab uprising: Country by countryhttp://www.bbc.com/news/world-12482311. Accessed 14 Dec 2019

BBC News (2019) Sudan crisis: What you need to know https://www.bbc.com/news/world-africa-48511226. Accessed 18 Dec 2019

BBC News (2015) "Omar al-Bashir wins Sudan elections by a landslide". Retrieved 18 Dec 2019.

Dionne, Kim Yi (2018) Are protests in Africa politically or economically https://www.washingtonpost.com/news/monkey-cage/wp/2018/08/24/are-protests-in-africa-politically-or-economically-motivated-this-new-book-has-answers/. Accessed 14 Dec 2019

Darboe, K Mustapha (2019) Gambia: Protesters call for president's resignation https://www.aa.com.tr/en/africa/gambia-protesters-call-for-president-s-resignation/1675442. Accessed 18 Dec 2019

Dodoo, Lennart (2019) Liberia: Associate Justice Ja'neh Lawyers Want Impeachment Trial Dismissed. https://frontpageafricaonline.com/front-slider/liberia-associate-justice-janeh-lawyers-want-impeachment-trial-dismissed/. Accessed 20 Dec 2019

Dodoo, Lennart (2019) June 7 'Save the State' Protest Ends in Deadlock, Poised to Continue on Monday. https://frontpageafricaonline.com/amp/news/liberia-june-7-save-the-state-protest-ends-in-deadlock-poised-to-continue-on-monday/. Accessed 24 July 2020

Davis, Abednego (2019) Reprisal Replacement? https://www.liberianobserver.com/news/reprisal-replacement/ Accessed 21 Dec 2019.

Dopoe, Robin (2020) Liberia: CoP Insists On January 6 for Protest https://allafrica.com/stories/202001030329.html. Accessed 24 July 2020

Doubek, James (2019) Algerian President Abdelaziz Bouteflika Resigns Early Under Pressure. https://www.npr.org/2019/04/03/709340831/algerian-president-abdelaziz-bouteflika-resigns-early-under-pressure. Accessed 21 Dec 2019

Davies, Wyre (2010). "Tunisia: President Zine al-Abidine Ben Ali forced out". BBC News. Archived from the original on 15 January 2011. Accessed 21 Dec 2019

France24 (2019) Sudan's new cabinet sworn in as nation transitions to civilian rule https://www.france24.com/en/20190908-sudans-new-cabinet-sworn-nation-transitions-civilian-rule. Accessed 18 Dec 2019

Frintz, Anne (2014) The fall of Blaise Compaoré https://mondediplo.com/2014/12/10burkina. Accessed 24 June 2020

Guliyev, Farid (2009) Monarchical Presidencies on the Rise. Harvard International Review http://www.harvardir.org/. Accessed 23 Dec 2019

The Guardian (2019) DRC court confirms Felix Tshisekedi winner of presidential election https://www.theguardian.com/world/2019/jan/20/drc-court-confirms-felix-tshisekedi-winner-of-presidential-election. Accessed 19 Dec 2019

The Guardian (2019) Guinea protests turn bloody in fight to stop president's third term https://www.theguardian.com/global-development/2019/dec/17/guinea-protests-turn-bloody-in-fight-to-stop-presidents-third-term. Accessed 19 Dec 2019.

Global Post/AFP (2016) "Ugandan election commission lacks 'independence': EU observers". Retrieved 2019-`12-19.

Geterminah, Hannah (2019) "General Power" Leads Roots FM Shutdown https://www.liberianobserver.com/news/general-power-leads-roots-fmshutdown/. Accessed 24 July 2020

Gathara, Patrick (2019) Electoral fraud and fake democracies are a global problem https://www.ft.com/content/1abd7fde-20b4-11e9-a46f-08f9738d6b2b Accessed 19 Dec 2019

Guinea (2019) Crackdown on Right to Protest Threats to Opposition Freedoms as President Considers Controversial Third Term https://www.hrw.org/news/2019/10/03/guinea-crackdown-right-protest. Accessed 16 Dec 2019

Hardy, Roger (2011). "Egypt protests: an Arab spring as old order crumbles". BBC. Archived from the original on 22 March 2011. Retrieved 9 Dec 2019.

Korotayev A; Zinkina J (2011). "Egyptian Revolution: A Demographic Structural Analysis". Entelequia. Revista. Interdisciplinar. 13: 139–165. Archived from the original on 20 October 2016.

Kerr, Nicholas & Lührmann, Anna (2017) Public trust in elections: The role of media freedom and election management autonomy. Working Paper No.

170. Afrobarometer Khadiagala, Gilbert m. (2011) Fraudulent Elections Lead to? Pseudo-Democracy- How Can the Crisis of Democracy be Overcome in Africa

Krippahl Cristina & Seagbeh. Evelyn Kpadeh (2020) Liberians rally in anti-government protest. https://www.dw.com/en/liberians-rally-in-anti-government-protest/a-51833744. Accessed 21 Jan 2020.

Kindzeka, Moki Edwin (2018) Cameroon's Biya Declared Election Winner https://www.voanews.com/africa/cameroons-biya-declared-election-winner. Accessed 21 Jan 2020

Laskar, Manzoor Elahi (2013) Summary of Social Contract Theory by Hobbes, Lock and Rousseau. file:///C:/Users/PC-!/AppData/Local/Temp/SSRN-id2410525.pdf. Accessed 24 July 2020

Montesquieu and Madison (1788) Separation of Powers with Checks and Balances. https://www.docsoffreedom.org/student/readings/separation-of-powers-with-checks-and-balances. Accessed 21 Jan 2020

News Central (2019) Benin police restore calm after post-election protests https://newscentral.africa/benin-police-restore-calm-after-post-election-protests/. Accessed 23 Jan 2020

Parks, Cara (2011). "Libya Protests: Gaddafi Militia Opens Fire On demonstrators". Huffington Post. Archived from the original on 1 March 2011. Retrieved 18 Dec 2019.

Rouaba, Ahmed (2019) Algeria election: Thousands march to protest in Algiers https://www.bbc.com/news/world-africa-50717749 Accessed 14 Dec 2019

Smelser, Neil J (1963) Theory of Collective Behavior New York: The Free Press of Glencoe Salem, Fadi; Mourtada, Racha (2011). "Civil Movements: The Impact of Facebook and Twitter" (PDF). Retrieved 17 Dec 2019.

Signé, Landry (2018) Cameroon's contentious elections come at a precarious time in the country's history https://qz.com/africa/1416006/cameroon-election-2018-everything-you-need-to-know/Accessed 18 Dec 2019

Samb, Saliou (2019) At least two dead in Guinea protests against change to Constitution Sieh, Rodney (2019) US Lawmaker Red Flags 'Deterioration of Political Conditions' in Liberia. FrontPage Africa. Accessed 25 Dec 2019

Torchia, Christopher and Mutsaka, Farai (2017) Robert Mugabe resigns as Zimbabwe's president after 37 years. Associated Press https://www.gazettenet.com/Mugabe-resigns-13881965. Accessed 18 Dec 2019

Xinhua (2019) More violence in Malawi's post-election protests http://www.xinhuanet.com/english/2019-07/26/c_138258383.htm. Accessed 23 Jan 2020

ABOUT THE AUTHOR

Ambrues M. Nebo Sr. is currently a PhD candidate in Sociology, Atlantic International University, Honolulu, Hawaii USA. He holds a MSc in the top 5 % of the graduating Class in Peace and Conflict Studies form the Centre of Peace and Conflict Studies University of Ibadan, Nigeria, Post Graduate Certificate with distinction in Public Administration from Ghana Institute of Management and Public Administration Ghana, BA Hon (Magna Cum Laude) in Sociology from African Methodist Episcopal Zion University College in Liberia and various International Certificates in peacekeeping operations from the Kofi Anna International Peacekeeping Training Centre in Ghana.

He is also a part-time lecturer in the Department of Sociology, African Methodist Episcopal University, Criminal Justice Department, Adventist University of West Africa, Liberia and Department of Political Science, University of Liberia.

Professionally, he is a senior police officer of the Liberia National Police with fifteen years of experience in training and administration.

Besides this book, he has authored his first book caption 'The Politicization of the Criminal Justice System: A Liberian Perspective
He also authored a dozen of articles dealing with contemporary issues in Africa and Liberia. Some of the articles that can be accessed online through neboambrues.academia.edu. includes: The Dark side of Majority Rule in Africa; Legitimatizing the illegitimate: Another Game in Politics; Sociological Analysis on the Culture of Silence; a feature of Prolonged Regime in Africa; The Gambia Military Coup Confirms Theory, My Fears for Christianizing Liberia; The Roles of the Government in Social Stratification; Sociological Perspectives on Nightclubs; Africa withdrawal from the International Criminal Court is not a guarantee for escape routes; Sociological Analysis of Vote Buying in Liberia.